DEPENDING ON JESUS

DISCOVERING THE SUFFICIENCY OF CHRIST

DALE & SANDY LARSEN

10 STUDIES
FOR INDIVIDUALS
OR GROUPS

Life
Builder
Study

INTER-VARSITY PRESS
36 Causton Street, London SW1P 4ST, England
Email: ivp@ivpbooks.com
Website: www.ivpbooks.com

Originally published in the United States of America in the LifeGuide® Bible Studies series in 2019 by InterVarsity Press, Downers Grove, Illinois
This edition published in Great Britain by Inter-Varsity Press 2019

British Library Cataloguing-in-Publication Data
A catalogue record for this book is available from the British Library.

ISBN: 978-1-78974-112-4
eBook ISBN: 978-1-78974-113-1

Inter-Varsity Press publishes Christian books that are true to the Bible and that communicate the gospel, develop discipleship and strengthen the church for its mission in the world.

IVP originated within the Inter-Varsity Fellowship, now the Universities and Colleges Christian Fellowship, a student movement connecting Christian Unions in universities and colleges throughout Great Britain, and a member movement of the International Fellowship of Evangelical Students. Website: www.uccf.org.uk. That historic association is maintained, and all senior IVP staff and committee members subscribe to the UCCF Basis of Faith.

CONTENTS

GETTING THE
MOST OUT OF
DEPENDING ON JESUS

I 've learned I have to depend on Jesus for everything."
That is what a friend going through a rough time said to us. It was
an extreme statement. It sounded almost too radical.

Of course believers know we have to depend on Jesus for many
things: for salvation, for guidance, for forgiveness, for daily needs.

But to depend on him for *everything*? Excluding nothing? It was a
scary idea. It was also, we realized, a profoundly biblical idea.

Some time later we spotted a sign in the back window of a pickup
truck: "Jesus Is Enough." (We must have a thing for noticing signs.
The idea for our LifeBuilder Bible study guides *Questions God Asks* and
Questions Jesus Asks came from a sign we saw in front of a church.) The
bottom of the sign was cut off from view by the truck's tailgate. Did it say
more? Did it say, Jesus is enough . . . for me? enough for you? enough
to get me through today? Or did it say only "Jesus is enough," period?

The truck drove on, and we never found out if there was more to the
sign. But as we worked on this study guide and lived with the realities
we found in Scripture, the truth came home to us more and more that
our friend was right, that Jesus *is* enough—for everything. What are the
alternatives? To depend on ourselves, our own smarts, our own schemes,
our own power of influence? To depend on other people who are as
fallible as we are? Ultimately all those options come up short and will
leave us disappointed.

Biblical people who followed Christ encountered every kind of ob-
stacle: hostility, loneliness, injustice, failure, and other seemingly impossible difficulties. In this study are ten instances of biblical people
learning that they could rely on Christ to see them through, even when
all other avenues of help failed. Just as they discovered that Christ is

sufficient for any and all circumstances, we pray that you will be encouraged to discover the same.

And as we thanked whoever put up the sign in front of the church that sparked those other two study guides, we thank the person who stuck that sign in the back window of a truck. Your influence will go further than you imagined.

SUGGESTIONS FOR INDIVIDUAL STUDY

1. As you begin each study, pray that God will speak to you through his Word.

2. Read the introduction to the study and respond to the personal reflection question or exercise. This is designed to help you focus on God and on the theme of the study.

3. Each study deals with a particular passage so that you can delve into the author's meaning in that context. Read and re-read the passage to be studied. The questions are written using the language of the New International Version, so you may wish to use that version of the Bible. The New Revised Standard Version is also recommended.

4. This is an inductive Bible study, designed to help you discover for yourself what Scripture is saying. The study includes three types of questions. Observation questions ask about the basic facts: who, what, when, where, and how. Interpretation questions delve into the meaning of the passage. Application questions help you discover the implications of the text for growing in Christ. These three keys unlock the treasures of Scripture.

Write your answers to the questions in the spaces provided or in a personal journal. Writing can bring clarity and deeper understanding of yourself and of God's Word.

5. It might be good to have a Bible dictionary handy. Use it to look up any unfamiliar words, names, or places.

6. Use the prayer suggestion to guide you in thanking God for what you have learned and to pray about the applications that have come to mind.

7. You may want to go on to the suggestion under "Now or Later," or you may want to use that idea for your next study.

SUGGESTIONS FOR MEMBERS OF A GROUP STUDY

1. Come to the study prepared. Follow the suggestions for individual study mentioned above. You will find that careful preparation will greatly enrich your time spent in group discussion.

2. Be willing to participate in the discussion. The leader of your group will not be lecturing. Instead, he or she will be encouraging the members of the group to discuss what they have learned. The leader will be asking the questions that are found in this guide.

3. Stick to the topic being discussed. Your answers should be based on the verses that are the focus of the discussion and not on outside authorities such as commentaries or speakers. These studies focus on a particular passage of Scripture. Only rarely should you refer to other portions of the Bible. This allows for everyone to participate in in-depth study on equal ground.

4. Be sensitive to the other members of the group. Listen attentively when they describe what they have learned. You may be surprised by their insights! Each question assumes a variety of answers. Many questions do not have "right" answers, particularly questions that aim at meaning or application. Instead the questions push us to explore the passage more thoroughly.

When possible, link what you say to the comments of others. Also, be affirming whenever you can. This will encourage some of the more hesitant members of the group to participate.

5. Be careful not to dominate the discussion. We are sometimes so eager to express our thoughts that we leave too little opportunity for others to respond. By all means participate! But allow others to also.

6. Expect God to teach you through the passage being discussed and through the other members of the group. Pray that you will have an enjoyable and profitable time together, but also that as a result of the study you will find ways that you can take action individually or as a group.

7. Remember that anything said in the group is considered confidential and should not be discussed outside the group unless specific permission is given to do so.

8. If you are the group leader, you will find additional suggestions at the back of the guide.

ONE

STRENGTH WITHIN POWERLESSNESS

2 Corinthians 12:6-10

W e slid right through our gate and down the hill onto the highway!" Those were our friends' first words when they arrived at church. At the time of year we usually have snow, instead there had been a night of freezing rain. Roads, driveways, sidewalks, and the church parking lot were slick with ice.

Unexpected difficulties can make us feel like we're skidding on ice. Brakes are useless; the steering wheel has no effect; our confident sense of control is lost and we are powerless to save ourselves.

The apostle Paul desperately pleaded with the Lord to save him from a bad situation and received a surprising answer.

Group Discussion. Do you think most people in your society feel they have significant control over their lives, or not? Why do you answer as you do?

Personal Reflection. How well do you deal with situations in which you feel powerless?

Along with several fellow workers, Paul had established a Christian fellowship in the Greek city of Corinth (Acts 18). He wrote at least two and probably more letters to the Corinthian Christians. There were conflicts; some in the church were questioning his authority. In 2 Corinthians Paul defends his position as an apostle and asserts that God has entrusted him with the message of the gospel. While admitting his weaknesses, he refers to "a man in Christ" (apparently himself) who was caught up to heaven and had inexpressible visions. Then his tone changes. *Read 2 Corinthians 12:6-10.*

1. What attitude had Paul developed toward his weaknesses?

2. What danger did Paul see in the unique spiritual blessings he had been given?

3. Paul says that he was given "a thorn in my flesh" by God. What good could such a "thorn" accomplish?

4. Possible explanations for Paul's "thorn" are physical illness or disability, temptations to sin, and opposition to the gospel. For you, what sort of hardships would most quickly put a damper on your pride?

5. Consider Paul's repeated pleas in verse 8. What do you think they indicate about Paul and his relationship with Christ?

6. For you, what is the most powerful part of Christ's response to Paul (v. 9)?

7. When have you witnessed the power of Christ in weakness—your own or someone else's?

8. How did Christ's answer transform Paul's attitude toward his thorn (vv. 9-10)?

9. Christ's assurance to Paul in verse 9 is also timeless for all Christians. How can Christ's words transform your attitude toward the problem you identified in question 2?

10. Paul's list of difficulties in verse 10 is enough to discourage anyone. How could Paul "delight" in these?

11. What does it mean that Paul delighted in these weaknesses and difficulties "for Christ's sake" (v. 10)?

12. Maybe you long to say, with Paul, "When I am weak, then I am strong" (v. 10). To say that means to acknowledge your own weakness and accept the sufficiency of Christ's strength. In what situations or areas of life do you long to be able to do that?

13. What would you have to give up in order to find the strength of Christ that Paul found even in his weakness?

 Paul came to prefer seeing Christ at work in him over being relieved of the thorn in his flesh. Pray that you will find increasing joy and satisfaction in seeing the power of Christ at work in and through your own weaknesses.

NOW OR LATER

Study Matthew 26:36-46. In Gethsemane Jesus prays three times for the cup to be taken from him, yet he yields to the Father's will.

Think of someone you have seen Christ working in even as the person goes through difficulties. Send a message or call that person simply to say how he or she has encouraged you.

TWO

DIRECTION WITHIN FRUSTRATION

Acts 16:1-10

B efore we went into writing full-time, we experienced three frus-
trating years as Dale searched for God's will for a specific job. Many
times doors appeared to open, then were abruptly shut. We prayed, re-
searched diligently, traveled for interviews, and consulted knowl-
edgeable people. Finally, one night after a disappointing rejection letter,
Dale sat down on the bed and said, "Why don't we forget it all and just
go write?" Sandy thought that was the greatest idea she'd ever heard!

Why did it take us so long to get to that decision point? Would we
have been ready for that decision three years earlier? We still aren't sure.
But several decades later, we know it was the right decision.

After a time of fruitful ministry in Asia Minor, Paul, Silas, and Timothy
found their way blocked by the Holy Spirit. As they searched for the
right direction to go, they must have been mystified. What was going
on? What did the Lord want, and what was he doing?

Group Discussion. What are some good and bad ways that people deal
with frustration?

Personal Reflection. What are some unusual ways that the Lord has
led you?

In Antioch the Holy Spirit set aside Paul and Barnabas for the work
of spreading the gospel into the wider world (Acts 13:1-3). Accompanied
at first by John Mark, they set out and proclaimed Christ to both Jews
and Gentiles throughout Asia Minor (Acts 13–14). The fact that Gentiles
were turning to Christ led to a consultation in Jerusalem to decide

whether Gentile Christians needed to conform to Jewish law (Acts 15). Later, Paul proposed a return visit to the young Christian churches in Asia Minor. Disagreement over John Mark's desertion caused a rift between Paul and Barnabas. Paul chose Silas to accompany him, and they set off with the blessing of the Antioch church (Acts 15:36-41). Later they were joined by Timothy and Luke.

A map of Paul's missionary journeys, often found in Bibles, will be helpful for this study. *Read Acts 16:1-10.*

1. How would you describe Paul and Silas's journey in verses 1-5?

2. From apparent success, how did the missionaries' journey abruptly change in verses 6-8?

3. What questions about the Lord's sufficiency would reasonably arise in Paul and Silas's minds (and perhaps Timothy's also) at the circumstances in verses 6-8?

4. Recall times you have felt frustrated at being prevented from doing what you thought was the Lord's will for you. How did you pray during those times?

5. How did Christ show his sufficiency for the missionaries in the radical change that took place in Troas (vv. 9-10)?

6. A few brief sentences tell the story of the missionaries' travels in verses 6-8, but the journey consumed weeks as they traveled hundreds of miles on foot. The Holy Spirit could have told them to go to Troas—even to cross over to Macedonia—while they were still in Derbe or Lystra (Acts 16:1). What value can you see in the Holy Spirit's delay in guiding them to Macedonia?

7. Think again of the times you recalled in question 4. What did you learn through the experience of waiting for guidance?

8. After Paul received the vision, what was the missionaries' responsibility?

9. While visions such as Paul's do happen, the Lord usually guides in other less dramatic ways. What principles do you use to determine the Lord's leading?

10. Right now, in what area(s) of your life do you need clearer direction?

11. When Paul and his companions were blocked from ministering in one area, they tried other places. How can you follow their example of investigating possibilities even while waiting for guidance?

 Pray that you will believe with heart and mind that the Lord is fully able to guide you in the way he wants. Pray also for courage to go ahead when the way is clear.

NOW OR LATER

Consider again your responses to questions 10 and 11. Find objects to represent those areas in which you want clearer direction from the Lord. Any objects will do. Place them where you will see them often and let them remind you of the assurance of guidance as well as your need to be aware of how the Lord might be guiding you.

THREE

REST WITHIN WORK

Matthew 11:28-30

F or several years Sandy worked temporary secretarial jobs in business offices. As a writer, she was irritated that she spent her days typing other people's bad writing. She had no status to suggest rewording or to offer to rewrite anything. The work felt pointless, except for the hourly pay, which was not stellar. Sometimes she found ways to minister to her work colleagues, who often talked freely with her because they knew she would be gone in a week or so. On the whole, however, she found her temp jobs draining rather than satisfying.

Work is, well, *work*. When Jesus invites the work-weary to come to him and rest, we doubt if he means we should all go on permanent vacation. Then we should explore what he does mean by "rest."

Group Discussion. How do you feel about work (whatever form "work" takes for you)?

Personal Reflection. When have you experienced work as refreshing and restorative?

Severe warnings and profound reassurances are the immediate context of Jesus' welcoming words here. He has denounced "the towns in which most of his miracles had been performed, because they did not repent" (Matthew 11:20). Then "at that time" he praises his Father for revealing his wisdom to "little children" and for the intimacy he enjoys with his Father (Matthew 11:25-27). After he declares his exclusive relationship with the Father, he invites the weary and burdened to come to him. Later there will be an encounter with the Pharisees over rigid application of the Sabbath law (Matthew 12:1-8). *Read Matthew 11:28-30.*

1. In this brief passage, what does Christ offer?

2. What part does Christ play, and what part do the "weary and burdened" play?

3. Think of some inadequate ways people try to find rest. Why are those attempts unsatisfying?

4. In what ways do you feel (or have you felt) "weary and burdened"?

5. When Jesus promises rest, we can assume he does not mean, abandon all your responsibilities, ditch your commitments, and live on the beach. Then how can a follower of Christ receive rest in the midst of diligent activity?

6. Taking the "yoke" of Jesus (v. 29) seems to contradict accepting rest from him. How might those two ideas be reconciled?

7. Along with the call to take on his yoke, Jesus calls his followers to "learn" from him (v. 29). Why is learning from him a necessary part of taking on his yoke?

8. How can being "gentle and humble in heart" (v. 29) be characteristics of strength?

9. Think of various forms that the "yoke" of Jesus has taken in your life. In what senses have you found Christ's yoke "easy" and his burden "light" (v. 30)?

10. How can a Christian believer discern the difference between doing good works through self-effort or for the wrong reasons, and doing good works out of trust and love for Christ?

11. In what areas do you feel the strain or even exhaustion of self-effort, even in what you know are good and worthwhile involvements?

12. Christ promises that he is sufficient to provide rest for our souls even in the midst of work. What are some practical ways you can "come" to him in the midst of your work and accept his rest?

13. How will you put those ways into practice this coming week?

 Pray that you will not overlook the opportunities the Lord gives you for both physical and spiritual rest.

NOW OR LATER

Hebrews 4:10 declares that those who enter God's rest are able to rest from their own works. Study Hebrews 4:1-11 concerning the promise of entering God's rest.

FOUR

RENEWAL WITHIN DEFEAT

Luke 24:13-35

E ven though Sandy had seldom run five miles at a stretch, she decided to enter a five-mile race. At the starter's signal she took off with a pack of male runners and kept up with them for a mile or so. Then she fell hopelessly behind. By the time she struggled across the finish line, she wondered why she had bothered to enter the race at all. Imagine her shock when she was handed a first-place trophy! The reason: all the other women in the race had dropped out or chosen to walk the route instead of run, so Sandy was the first female finisher. Obvious defeat had turned into unexpected (though hardly well-earned) victory.

Who could feel more defeated than Jesus' followers after his death? Two of them discussed their dashed hopes as they trudged home from Jerusalem. Then a stranger joined them and revolutionized their outlook.

Group Discussion. When and how has discouragement changed into encouragement for you?

Personal Reflection. When have you felt defeated with no place to turn? If the situation has been resolved, what was the outcome?

A group of women carry spices to Jesus' tomb expecting to anoint his dead body. Instead they meet angels who tell them that Jesus has risen. They run and tell the apostles and others, who think they are talking nonsense, although Peter goes to the tomb to check it out. Later that day, two discouraged followers of Jesus are walking from Jerusalem to the village of Emmaus and talking over the gut-wrenching events of the past few days. *Read Luke 24:13-35.*

1. What makes the resurrection of Jesus hard for people to believe?

2. In the city of Jerusalem, Jesus' followers had been told that Jesus was alive again, risen from the dead. What can you conclude from the fact that these two people left the company of disciples in Jerusalem and headed home to Emmaus?

3. The two travelers gave the inquiring stranger a concise summary of Jesus' life and death, including the women's report that he was alive again (vv. 15-24). Based on their appearance and words, how had they found "Jesus of Nazareth" to be *in*sufficient, that is, not living up to their expectations?

4. Why did Jesus call his two companions "foolish" and "slow to believe" (vv. 25-26)?

5. Although Jesus had not yet identified himself to the travelers, how did he demonstrate that "the Messiah" had fulfilled all that was prophesied about him (vv. 25-27)?

6. What effect should Jesus' review of the prophecies about the Messiah have had on the two travelers?

7. How did the simple act of sharing a meal turn into a moment of revelation (vv. 28-31)?

8. Looking back, what clues had the two disciples already received about their companion's identity (v. 32)?

9. How did realizing that Jesus was alive transform the lives of the two disciples (vv. 33-35)?

10. What difference do you think it makes whether Jesus is alive today or not?

11. In your own life, what difference(s) has it made to know that Jesus rose from the dead and is alive today?

12. Because Jesus lives, he is sufficient for any need that comes up in your life this week (and beyond). This coming week, how will you keep reminding yourself of that reality?

 Pray that you will stand secure in Christ's victory over death and over every other human sorrow.

NOW OR LATER

Study 1 Corinthians 15, in which Paul contrasts what would be true if Christ has *not* been raised and what is true because he *has* been raised.

FIVE

HELP WITHIN HOSTILITY

2 Corinthians 4:7-18

S ome forty years ago we bought a set of English bone china dinner-ware. Over the years we have purchased more pieces because we wanted to add to the set, not because the original pieces have gotten broken. Contrary to its fragile image, bone china is tough stuff. If we had bought earthenware dishes years ago, we would have gone through several sets by now.

The clay of earthenware is not very sturdy and is easily chipped or broken. Paul was not ashamed to write that we Christians carry the treasure of the gospel in easily broken clay jars. We are fragile, but Christ is unbreakable.

Group Discussion. When you face pressures from the society around you, what good things can result?

Personal Reflection. When have you felt most fragile?

In 2 Corinthians 4:1-6 Paul defends his and his associates' integrity and their aim to promote not themselves but Jesus Christ as Lord. He confidently affirms that God "made his light shine in our hearts to give us the light of the knowledge of God's glory displayed in the face of Christ" (v. 6). Then in a passage of contrast beginning with, "But . . . " Paul's tone changes as he acknowledges the pressure of opposition. *Read 2 Corinthians 4:7-18.*

1. In the sharp contrasts Paul draws in this passage, what surprises you most?

2. How can people be likened to earthenware jars (v. 7)?

3. What does God accomplish by placing the treasure of the gospel in fragile human vessels?

4. Think of a time you observed someone (perhaps yourself) "hard pressed on every side, but not crushed; perplexed, but not in despair; persecuted, but not abandoned; struck down, but not destroyed" (vv. 8-9). How do you explain the person's resilience under the weight of such difficulties?

5. Paul writes that he and his associates carry around in their bodies the death of Jesus and are constantly given over to death for Jesus' sake (vv. 10-11). He means *living* Christians. How is this possible?

6. What is the result of such constant closeness with the death of Jesus (vv. 10-12)?

7. *Read 2 Corinthians 4:13-18.* In this passage what hopes does Paul affirm?

8. What is the connection between Jesus' resurrection and Paul's courage to speak out (vv. 13-15)?

9. How have you experienced being "renewed day by day" as Paul says in verse 16?

10. In what ways have afflictions altered the focus of Paul and his associates (vv. 17-18)?

11. "What is seen" often distracts us from "what is unseen" (v. 18). Why is this true?

12. In this coming week, what will you do to focus on "what is unseen" and live more fully in the hope that Christ offers you?

Think of situations in which you long to say, as Paul said of himself and his companions, "I do not lose heart." Bring those situations to Christ. Ask him to renew you day by day and give you hope, which is based not on circumstances but on his unchanging presence and love for you.

NOW OR LATER

In 2 Corinthians 4:17 Paul refers to his "light and momentary troubles." In 2 Corinthians 6:3-10 and 11:23-29 he enumerates some of those troubles. Study those passages, exploring how Paul could possibly call such difficulties "light and momentary."

Study John 16:31-33. Here Jesus predicts that his disciples will abandon him, yet he will not be alone, and he still offers them peace.

SIX

COURAGE WITHIN INJUSTICE

Acts 16:16-40

W hen US Supreme Court Chief Justice John Roberts addressed his son's ninth-grade graduating class, he offered some unconventional wishes, including these:

> From time to time in the years to come, I hope you will be treated unfairly, so that you will come to know the value of justice. I hope that you will suffer betrayal because that will teach you the importance of loyalty.... And when you lose, as you will from time to time, I hope every now and then, your opponent will gloat over your failure. It is a way for you to understand the importance of sportsmanship.*

The followers of Jesus Christ frequently meet and endure injustice and disloyalty. The apostle Paul and his companions often found themselves treated unfairly. And of course Jesus himself, innocent of any sin or crime, received the most unjust treatment of all.

Group Discussion. What makes something unjust?

Personal Reflection. How do you respond to injustice against others? Against yourself?

After the events related in study two, Paul and his companions sailed to Macedonia and began to share their message with a group of women in Philippi. A businesswoman named Lydia was converted to Christ and opened her home to the missionaries. Things soon turned troublesome.

As this and the following studies show, the Bible takes demons and demon possession seriously. *Read Acts 16:16-40.*

1. Up to this point, the work of Paul and his companions in Philippi had gone smoothly. How does the encounter in verses 16-18 reveal the spiritual conflict going on behind the scenes?

2. The spirit-possessed girl kept shouting, "These men are servants of the Most High God, who are telling you the way to be saved" (v. 17). What she said was certainly true. Why then did Paul command the spirit to come out of her (v. 18)?

3. Once the girl was delivered of the evil spirit, a cascade of injustices followed one after another (vv. 19-24). Theologian N. T. Wright says of these events that "the combination of religion, money and politics is asking for trouble, and Paul and Silas got it."** How were the missionaries subjected to unfairness through each of those three forces?

Religious

Financial

Political

4. Locked in prison at midnight, Paul and Silas could not know that the Lord would intervene on their behalf through an earthquake. How did their behavior in the prison demonstrate trust in the Lord both before and after the earthquake (vv. 25-28)?

5. In prison Paul and Silas did two things that have always helped Christians in bad circumstances: they prayed and sang hymns to God (v. 25). When have prayer and singing sustained you when life seemed unfair?

6. Earlier in the day, a cascade of injustices had followed the deliverance of the slave girl. What cascade of good now happened because Paul and Silas did not flee from prison and abandon the jailer (vv. 29-34)?

7. Paul and Silas had submitted to the injustices of the day before. How was their attitude different the next morning when they were told that they were free to go (vv. 35-37)?

8. What was the value of Paul's demand for fair treatment for the missionaries (a public apology and official stamp of approval) (vv. 38-40)?

9. How are you being unfairly treated right now?

10. How is someone you care about being unfairly treated right now?

11. What are some appropriate responses to both your situation and the situation of that person you care about?

12. This week, what will you do to put those responses into action?

 Commit the injustices of your life to the Lord, trusting him to work justice for you in his own time. Pray for courage to seek justice for others who are being unfairly treated.

NOW OR LATER

Study 2 Peter 2:11-25 concerning Christlike behavior in the face of unfair treatment.

---

*John Roberts, commencement address, Cardigan Mountain School, Canaan, NH, June 3, 2017, quoted in Katie Reilly, "I Wish You Bad Luck," *Time*, July 5, 2017, http://time.com/4845150/chief-justice-john-roberts-commencement-speech-transcript.

**N. T. Wright, *Acts for Everyone, Part Two: Chapters 13-18*, New Testament for Everyone (Louisville, KY: Westminster John Knox, 2011), 65.

SEVEN

RESTORATION WITHIN RUIN

Mark 5:1-20

O ur antique floor-model Edison phonograph cost $1. We found it in a garage sale, dirty, moldy, its veneer peeling, three of its four legs partly rotted off. However, its internal works were all there and in good condition: turntable, tone arm, speed control, crank, internal horn, even a wool record cleaning pad and bamboo needles, plus a drawerful of seventy-eight records. We hauled it home (it weighs about two hundred pounds) and Dale began to restore its outside. He reglued and replaced veneer, carved new legs to match the one existing leg, and stained and varnished the entire exterior. Furniture experts argue about whether an antique piece should be restored. For our phonograph, otherwise doomed to the junk heap, restoration saved its life.

Jesus met many people who one way or another were headed for the junk heap. He had compassion on them and mercifully restored them to full and meaningful life.

Group Discussion. What are some reasons people feel despair?

Personal Reflection. What gives you hope even in seemingly hopeless situations?

As study six showed, the Bible takes for granted that demons are real. The Gospels assume that demons, also called impure spirits, can take possession of people and cause violent and self-destructive behavior. Jesus is consistently more powerful than demons, and they are consistently in terror of him. By the time of this encounter in Mark's Gospel, Jesus has already built up a reputation of publicly casting out evil spirits (Mark 1:21-28, 34; 3:22). He speaks to demons with authority, and although they protest loudly, they have no power to resist him. The night before the encounter of this study, Jesus has shown his lordship over nature by calming a storm on the Sea of Galilee. Now his boat comes ashore in the Gentile region of the Decapolis. *Read Mark 5:1-20.*

1. Put yourself in the position of one of Jesus' disciples in this scene. As you get out of your boat, what do you see and hear (vv. 1-5)?

2. Still reacting as one of the disciples, what do you do as the possessed man approaches?

3. Identify all the ways this man's life appeared hopelessly ruined (vv. 1-5).

4. When have you felt that your cherished plans or dreams have been ruined by forces outside of your control?

5. How did everything change when Jesus came on the scene (vv. 6-7)?

6. As terrible as the scene appears in verses 6-10, how did it introduce new hope to the demon-possessed man?

7. What words and phrases in verses 6-13 show Jesus' indisputable power over the demons?

8. Identify all the radical changes you see between the condition of the man in verses 2-5 and his condition in verse 15.

9. Consider the reaction of the herdsmen and the local residents (vv. 14-17). Why do you think they missed the point of the miraculous deliverance Jesus had just accomplished for this man?

10. No doubt the newly delivered man was disappointed when Jesus refused to let him get into the boat (v.18). What did Jesus give him as a new aim for his life (vv. 19-20)?

11. In what area(s) of your life do you feel you are up against forces stronger than you are?

12. This week, how will you remind yourself that Christ is stronger than those forces that threaten your ruin?

 Admit to the Lord that there are things you just can't handle and that you do not know what to do about them, or even what you could do about them. Turn these things over to him and remain expectant for his answers.

NOW OR LATER

Study Psalm 35, David's plea that the Lord will "fight against those who fight against me" (v. 1) and his expression of confidence that "you rescue the poor from those too strong for them, the poor and needy from those who rob them" (v. 10). Make Psalm 35 your prayer for deliverance from ungodly adversaries, whether human or spiritual.

EIGHT

BELONGING WITHIN LONELINESS

2 Timothy 4:9-22

High school yearbooks traditionally feature prominent photos of senior class members, accompanied by lists of their school activities. Some seniors have seven or eight lines of club memberships, while others show only one organization or maybe none. Multiple lines may indicate that the student was a leader. On the other hand, they may indicate only that the student was a "joiner" who signed up for club after club simply from a need to belong.

We all want to belong, but the sensation of belonging may have nothing to do with how many clubs we join or how many people we have around us. Belonging is deeper than mere association. Even in a Roman prison, Paul experienced the reality of belonging to Christ and to his fellow believers.

Group Discussion. What are some things that give people a sense of belonging?

Personal Reflection. What has given you the deepest sense of belonging?

So far as we know, 2 Timothy is the last letter Paul wrote. Imprisoned in Rome under the persecution of Emperor Nero, he believed that his life was near its end. He wrote to Timothy, a young believer who had become one of his missionary traveling partners (Acts 16:1-3). Paul was very close to Timothy, addressing him in his letters as "my true son in the faith" (1 Timothy 1:2) and "my dear son" (2 Timothy 1:2). This letter is an open door into Paul's heart toward the end of his life. *Read 2 Timothy 4:9-22.*

1. Paul wrote this letter while imprisoned in Rome. On a Bible map, trace the various places his companions have been scattered.

2. In verse 9, Paul urgently pleads for Timothy to come to him. What reasons do verses 10-15 offer for that plea?

3. Consider the requests in verse 13. What do they reveal about Paul's physical and emotional condition?

4. What legitimate reasons would Paul have to feel abandoned?

5. When have you felt abandoned, so you can identify with Paul's experience?

6. When have you felt that you belonged, even when you were alone?

7. How does Paul express trust in the Lord concerning those who have opposed and deserted him (vv. 14-16)?

8. The Lord stood by Paul and strengthened him so he could continue proclaiming the gospel to the Gentiles (v. 17). How does seeing God's purposes in your life help you cope with a sense of being alone?

9. When have you been most keenly aware that you belong to Christ?

10. How does Paul's ultimate hope (v. 18) reveal his certainty that he belongs to Christ?

11. What gives you the greatest certainty that you belong to Christ?

12. If any sense of being abandoned hits you this week (or further in the future), what will be your strategy for coping with it?

 Honestly express to the Lord your need for belonging and any feelings you have that you do not belong. Pray for an ever increasing certainty that you belong unshakably to Christ.

NOW OR LATER

Study Psalms 41–44, prayers of people who reach out to God in the face of abandonment and betrayal.

NINE

EMPATHY WITHIN FALTERING

Hebrews 4:14–5:10

Y ou're going through hard times, relationship problems, physical illness, grief, or some other difficulty, and someone says, "I know just how you feel." You think, *No, you don't.* It's impossible for one person to know precisely how another person feels. Yet the offered empathy is more believable if you know that the other person has experienced *something* at least *somewhat* similar to what you are experiencing.

Scripture assures us that Jesus understands us because he actually has experienced all that we experience. He did not stay aloof from our frail human condition but freely entered into our brokenness—yet without succumbing to sin.

Group Discussion. What are some ways people show empathy for others?

Personal Reflection. Who is the most empathetic person you know? What are some ways that person shows empathy for others?

This passage begins with the word *therefore*, indicating that it flows naturally from what has come before. The writer has been expounding to Jewish Christians the many ways that Christ is superior to Moses and that Christ is the ultimate fulfillment of everything in the Jewish law. *Read Hebrews 4:14–5:10.*

1. Throughout this passage, what are the ways Jesus serves as believers' high priest?

2. Reading only verse 14, we would get the impression of Christ as high above us ordinary weak mortals. How do verses 15-16 assure us that we can confidently approach God?

3. The Gospels of Matthew, Mark, and Luke all record that Jesus was tempted by Satan in the desert after his baptism (Matthew 4:1-11; Mark 1:12-13; Luke 4:1-13). Certainly those were not the only times he was tempted during his earthly life. What other temptations would Jesus have endured (v. 15)?

4. What are the differences between the human high priest and Christ (vv. 1-4)?

5. How does God validate Christ as high priest (vv. 5-6)?

6. Jesus "offered up prayers and petitions with fervent cries and tears" in Gethsemane before he was arrested (Matthew 26:36-46; Mark 14:32-42; Luke 22:39-46) and no doubt at other times "during the days of [his] life on earth" (v. 7). When have you prayed with something like that intensity, and how did God answer?

7. Jesus was already the perfect and holy Son of God. Yet when he became incarnate as a human being, he had to learn "obedience from what he suffered" and be made perfect (vv. 8-9). How does that fact give you confidence that he understands and empathizes with you in your own struggles?

8. What are the results of Jesus' faithful obedience (vv. 8-10)?

9. Consider ways that you have faltered in faith or obedience. Where do you most need the assurance that Jesus empathizes with your weaknesses?

10. What will you do this week to stay aware that you are not alone in your weakness, but Christ understands and is ready to help you?

"Let us then approach God's throne of grace with confidence, so that we may receive mercy and find grace to help us in our time of need" (Hebrews 4:16). As you pray, approach God with confidence, ask for what you need, and accept his gracious help.

NOW OR LATER

Study what the book of Hebrews goes on to say about the priest Melchizedek in Hebrews 6:20–7:28.

TEN

MERCY WITHIN FAILURE

John 18:15-18, 25-27; 21:15-19

S ome people have no conscience, or at least it seems like it. Others of us have consciences that won't shut up. We keep mentally going over our mistakes: *If only I hadn't said that . . . If only I hadn't done that . . . If only I had said that or had done that . . . But I failed. Yes, I knew Christ was sufficient to help me, but I didn't avail myself of his help and now all is lost.* Or is it?

Peter professed absolute loyalty to his Lord, promising to go with him even to death. Shortly afterward Peter lied and said he did not even know Jesus. Who could forgive failure like that and restore such a person to fellowship and useful life again? Only Jesus himself, the very one Peter had so miserably failed.

Group Discussion. What are some good and bad ways people cope with failure?

Personal Reflection. Recall a time you overcame failure. How did it happen?

Despite Peter's bold proclamations of faithfulness, Jesus predicted that Peter would deny him three times that same night (John 13:36-38). The disciples scattered when Jesus was arrested (Mark 14:50), but Peter and another disciple returned and followed the arresting party to the home of the high priest. *Read John 18:15-18, 25-27.*

1. Despite having fled earlier, how did Peter show that he still felt loyal to Jesus (vv. 15-18)?

2. At the same time, how did Peter show disloyalty to Jesus (v. 17)?

3. How do you account for the discrepancy between Peter's actions and his words?

4. Imagine that you are Peter immediately after you answer the girl's question (v. 17). What is going through your mind and heart at that moment?

5. Still thinking of yourself as Peter, at that moment, what does your future look like?

6. In verses 19-24 the scene shifts to the home of Annas, the Jewish high priest. There Jesus maintained his dignity and his innocence in the face of humiliating interrogation. He was sent on to Caiaphas. The Gospel scene reverts to Peter warming himself beside the court-yard fire. What words and phrases would you use for Peter's replies to the questions he was asked (vv. 25-27)?

7. The rooster crowed after Peter denied Jesus for the third time, just as Jesus had predicted (John 13:36-38). Two other Gospels report that Peter "went outside and wept bitterly" (Matthew 26:75; Luke 22:62). Probably you have not been in such an extreme situation as Peter, but you may have sometimes denied knowing Christ either by what you said or by what you did not say. Afterward, how did your emotions compare with those of Peter?

8. There are many ways we fail other people, whether family, friends, employers, employees, church members, even strangers we meet. How is failing other people actually failing Christ?

After Mary Magdalene reported that Jesus' tomb was empty, Peter and "the other disciple" ran to the tomb. During the following week, Jesus appeared to all the disciples, proving that he was alive again. Some time afterward, Peter and six other disciples went fishing on the Sea of Galilee, familiar territory for several of them. They caught nothing all night. Early in the morning Jesus appeared on the shore. He directed them to a miraculously large catch of fish, some of which they cooked and ate together. *Read John 21:15-19.*

9. Why do you think Jesus asked Peter three times, "Do you love me?"

10. How did Jesus assure Peter that he was forgiven and restored to his role as a disciple?

11. What hope does Peter's restoration give to Christians who have failed the Lord?

12. What hope does Peter's restoration give you?

13. This week, if you are tempted to beat yourself up or wallow in the knowledge of past failures, how will you use this study as a source of encouragement and reassurance?

 Thank the Lord for his mercy. Praise him that no matter how often or how badly you have failed him, he died for those sins and he lives to raise you up again.

NOW OR LATER

Study Psalm 51, David's prayer of repentance and renewed hope after Nathan confronted him about his sin with Bathsheba.

Look back over all the studies in this guide. What new insights have you gained about the all-sufficiency of Christ? In what areas of your life do you have more confidence that you can trust him? Where do you still need more of that confidence?

LEADER'S NOTES

My grace is sufficient for you.

2 CORINTHIANS 12:9

L eading a Bible discussion can be an enjoyable and rewarding experience. But it can also be scary—especially if you've never done it before. If this is your feeling, you're in good company. When God asked Moses to lead the Israelites out of Egypt, he replied, "Please send someone else" (Exodus 4:13)! It was the same with Solomon, Jeremiah, and Timothy, but God helped these people in spite of their weaknesses, and he will help you as well.

You don't need to be an expert on the Bible or a trained teacher to lead a Bible discussion. The idea behind these inductive studies is that the leader guides group members to discover for themselves what the Bible has to say. This method of learning will allow group members to remember much more of what is said than a lecture would.

These studies are designed to be led easily. As a matter of fact, the flow of questions through the passage from observation to interpretation to application is so natural that you may feel that the studies lead themselves. This study guide is also flexible. You can use it with a variety of groups—student, professional, neighborhood, or church groups. Each study takes forty-five to sixty minutes in a group setting.

There are some important facts to know about group dynamics and encouraging discussion. The suggestions listed below should enable you to effectively and enjoyably fulfill your role as leader.

PREPARING FOR THE STUDY

1. Ask God to help you understand and apply the passage in your own life. Unless this happens, you will not be prepared to lead others. Pray too for the various members of the group. Ask God to open your hearts to the message of his Word and motivate you to action.

2. Read the introduction to the guide to get an overview of the entire book and the issues that will be explored.

3. As you begin each study, read and re-read the assigned Bible passage to familiarize yourself with it.

4. This study guide is based on the New International Version of the Bible. It will help you and the group if you use this translation as the basis for your study and discussion.

5. Carefully work through each question in the study. Spend time in meditation and reflection as you consider how to respond.

6. Write your thoughts and responses in the space provided in the study guide. This will help you to express your understanding of the passage clearly.

7. It might help to have a Bible dictionary handy. Use it to look up any unfamiliar words, names, or places. (For additional help on how to study a passage, see chapter five of *How to Lead a LifeBuilder Study*, IVP, 2018.)

8. Consider how you can apply the Scripture to your life. Remember that the group will follow your lead in responding to the studies. They will not go any deeper than you do.

9. Once you have finished your own study of the passage, familiarize yourself with the leader's notes for the study you are leading. These are designed to help you in several ways. First, they tell you the purpose the study guide author had in mind when writing the study. Take time to think through how the study questions work together to accomplish that purpose. Second, the notes provide you with additional background information or suggestions on group dynamics for various questions. This information can be useful when people have difficulty understanding or answering a question. Third, the leader's notes can alert you to potential problems you may encounter during the study.

10. If you wish to remind yourself of anything mentioned in the leader's notes, make a note to yourself below that question in the study.

LEADING THE STUDY

1. Begin the study on time. Open with prayer, asking God to help the group to understand and apply the passage.

2. Be sure that everyone in your group has a study guide. Encourage the group to prepare beforehand for each discussion by reading the introduction to the guide and by working through the questions in the study.

3. At the beginning of your first time together, explain that these studies are meant to be discussions, not lectures. Encourage the members of the group to participate. However, do not put pressure on those who may be hesitant to speak during the first few sessions. You may want to suggest the following guidelines to your group.

- Stick to the topic being discussed.

- Your responses should be based on the verses that are the focus of the discussion and not on outside authorities such as commentaries or speakers.

- These studies focus on a particular passage of Scripture. Only rarely should you refer to other portions of the Bible. This allows for everyone to participate in in-depth study on equal ground.

- Anything said in the group is considered confidential and will not be discussed outside the group unless specific permission is given to do so.

- We will listen attentively to each other and provide time for each person present to talk.

- We will pray for each other.

4. Have a group member read the introduction at the beginning of the discussion.

5. Every session begins with a group discussion question. The question or activity is meant to be used before the passage is read. The question introduces the theme of the study and encourages group members to begin to open up. Encourage as many members as possible to participate, and be ready to get the discussion going with your own response.

This section is designed to reveal where our thoughts or feelings need to be transformed by Scripture. That is why it is especially important not to read the passage before the discussion question is asked. The passage will tend to color the honest reactions people would otherwise give because they are, of course, supposed to think the way the Bible does.

You may want to supplement the group discussion question with an icebreaker to help people get comfortable. See the community section of the *Small Group Starter Kit* (IVP, 1995) for more ideas.

You also might want to use the personal reflection question with your group. Either allow a time of silence for people to respond individually or discuss it together.

6. Have a group member (or members if the passage is long) read aloud the passage to be studied. Then give people several minutes to read the passage again silently so that they can take it all in.

7. Question 1 will generally be an overview question designed to briefly survey the passage. Encourage the group to look at the whole passage, but try to avoid getting sidetracked by questions or issues that will be addressed later in the study.

8. As you ask the questions, keep in mind that they are designed to be used just as they are written. You may simply read them aloud. Or you may prefer to express them in your own words.

There may be times when it is appropriate to deviate from the study guide. For example, a question may have already been answered. If so, move on to the next question. Or someone may raise an important question not covered in the guide. Take time to discuss it, but try to keep the group from going off on tangents.

9. Avoid answering your own questions. If necessary, repeat or rephrase them until they are clearly understood. Or point out something you read in the leader's notes to clarify the context or meaning. An eager group quickly becomes passive and silent if they think the leader will do most of the talking.

10. Don't be afraid of silence. People may need time to think about the question before formulating their answers.

11. Don't be content with just one answer. Ask, "What do the rest of you think?" or "Anything else?" until several people have given answers to the question.

12. Acknowledge all contributions. Try to be affirming whenever possible. Never reject an answer. If it is clearly off base, ask, "Which verse led you to that conclusion?" or again, "What do the rest of you think?"

13. Don't expect every answer to be addressed to you, even though this will probably happen at first. As group members become more at ease, they will begin to truly interact with each other. This is one sign of healthy discussion.

14. Don't be afraid of controversy. It can be very stimulating. If you don't resolve an issue completely, don't be frustrated. Move on and keep it in mind for later. A subsequent study may solve the problem.

15. Periodically summarize what the group has said about the passage. This helps to draw together the various ideas mentioned and gives continuity to the study. But don't preach.

16. At the end of the Bible discussion you may want to allow group members a time of quiet to work on an idea under "Now or Later." Then discuss what you experienced. Or you may want to encourage group members to work on these ideas between meetings. Give an opportunity during the session for people to talk about what they are learning.

17. Conclude your time together with conversational prayer, adapting the prayer suggestion at the end of the study to your group. Ask for God's help in following through on the commitments you've made.

18. End on time.

Many more suggestions and helps are found in *How to Lead a LifeBuilder Study.*

COMPONENTS OF SMALL GROUPS

A healthy small group should do more than study the Bible. There are four components to consider as you structure your time together.

Nurture. Small groups help us to grow in our knowledge and love of God. Bible study is the key to making this happen and is the foundation of your small group.

Community. Small groups are a great place to develop deep friendships with other Christians. Allow time for informal interaction before and after each study. Plan activities and games that will help you get to know each other. Spend time having fun together going on a picnic or cooking dinner together.

Worship and prayer. Your study will be enhanced by spending time praising God together in prayer or song. Pray for each other's needs and keep track of how God is answering prayer in your group. Ask God to help you to apply what you are learning in your study.

Outreach. Reaching out to others can be a practical way of applying what you are learning, and it will keep your group from becoming self-focused. Host a series of evangelistic discussions for your friends or neighbors. Clean up the yard of an elderly friend. Serve at a soup kitchen together, or spend a day working in the community.

Many more suggestions and helps in each of these areas are found in the *Small Group Starter Kit.* You will also find information on building a small group. Reading through the starter kit will be worth your time.

Before each study, you may want to put an asterisk by the key questions you think are most important for your group to cover, in case you don't have time to cover all the questions. As we suggested in "Getting the Most Out of *Depending on Jesus*," if you want to make sure you have enough time to discuss all the questions, you have other options. For example, the group could decide to extend each meeting to ninety minutes or more. Alternatively, you could devote two sixty-minute sessions to each study.

STUDY 1. STRENGTH WITHIN POWERLESSNESS. 2 CORINTHIANS 12:6-10.

PURPOSE: To increasingly rely on the strength of Christ to cope with seemingly impossible difficulties.

Question 3. According to the *Hard Sayings of the Bible*, three things can be said about Paul's "thorn." First, it was evil, a "messenger of Satan." Second, God allowed it. Third, it caused some kind of weakness in Paul. (Walter C. Kaiser Jr., Peter H. Davids, F. F. Bruce, and Manfred T. Brauch, *Hard Sayings of the Bible* [Downers Grove, IL: InterVarsity Press, 1996], 627-29)

Question 5. Paul's repeated prayers may demonstrate his honesty before the Lord, his desperation, and his persistent faith. They also show that Paul was not instantly reconciled to his difficulty. It took time for him to come to the point of acceptance.

Question 8. New Testament scholar Craig Keener observes,

In paganism, divine power was especially displayed in magical wonders; for Paul, it is God's power enabling one weak in himself to endure. Miracle reports in pagan temples often followed the same form as Paul's request (v. 8) but concluded with the deity's appearing to heal the person. Although Paul had performed many miracles (12:12), he would not boast in his miracles, as his opponents perhaps boasted in theirs; instead he boasts in his weakness. (Craig S. Keener, *The IVP Bible Background Commentary: New Testament* [Downers Grove, IL: InterVarsity Press, 1993], 514)

STUDY 2. DIRECTION WITHIN FRUSTRATION. ACTS 16:1-10.

PURPOSE: To become increasingly patient and sensitive to the means by which the Lord offers guidance.

Question 1. The first part of the journey appeared successful and blessed by God. Paul and Silas gained an associate Timothy whose family had a history of faith (2 Timothy 1:5). They passed along the decisions of the Jerusalem Council, and the churches were growing in both faith and numbers.

Paul's decision to have Timothy circumcised puzzles many readers of Acts.

No sooner does Acts report the Jerusalem Council's decision that it is not necessary for one to be circumcised or keep the Mosaic law to be saved (Acts 15) than it mentions Paul's circumcising Timothy in order to take him along as a coworker. . . .

When seen as a cultural rather than a religious issue, circumcision was an indifferent practice. Where it could be used for the advantage of the gospel, it was good. Where it hindered the gospel, it was to be avoided. In no case did it make the person more or less spiritual. (Kaiser et al., *Hard Sayings of the Bible*, 530-31)

Questions 2 and 3. The Holy Spirit blocked the missionaries' efforts to go into "the province of Asia" (the western end of modern Turkey) and Bithynia (the north part of modern Turkey). Acts does not say what form the roadblocks took, but clearly they were put up by God and not by enemies of the gospel.

The unique phrase *the Spirit of Jesus* may imply a vision of the Lord. On the other hand, Paul was travelling with Silas, a man known as a prophet (15:32), and the directions may have come through him. (Conrad Gempf, "Acts," *New Bible Commentary: 21st Century Edition*, ed. D. A. Carson, R. T. France, J. A. Motyer, G. J. Wenham [Downers Grove, IL: InterVarsity Press, 1994], 1089)

Question 5. Visions from the Lord took place at key times in the book of Acts. Besides Paul's vision of the Macedonian man, he experienced visions recorded in Acts 9:12, 18:9-10, 22:17-21, and 27:21-25, as well as his encounter with the risen Christ in Acts 9:3-6. Visions were also given to Ananias (Acts 9:6-10), Cornelius (Acts 10:1-6), and Peter (Acts 10:9-20).

Question 9. According to the *Dictionary of Biblical Imagery*,

The actual images by which God literally or metaphorically guides people are vivid and varied. He guides them by his unfailing love and his strength (Ex 15:13), with light and truth (Ps 43:3), with his counsel (Ps 73:24) and with his hand (Ps 139:10). God led Abraham's servant to the right wife for Isaac by an answered prayer (Gen 24:10-27) and Paul into Macedonia by a dream of a man saying, "Come over to Macedonia and help us" (Acts 16:9). He gave Gideon direction by means of a "fleece test" (Judg 6:36-40). We can find examples in the Bible of a range of ways in which God provides this guidance—through his revealed Word (with its moral guidance), the example and teachings of Jesus, the indwelling presence of the Holy Spirit, the influence of godly models (including spouses and parents), and the exhortations of spiritual leaders or advisers. ("Guide, Guidance," *Dictionary of Biblical Imagery*, ed. Leland Ryken, James C. Wilhoit, Tremper Longman III [Downers Grove, IL: InterVarsity Press, 1998], 355)

STUDY 3. REST WITHIN WORK. MATTHEW 11:28-30.

PURPOSE: To find refreshment in the service of Christ.

Question 3. Some translations have "all who labor" rather than "all who are weary." The Greek word "has the two different meanings (*a*) 'growing wearing,'(*b*) 'toiling;' it is sometimes translated 'to bestow labor'" ("Labor," in W. E. Vine, *Vine's Complete Expository Dictionary of Old and New Testament Words* [Nashville: Thomas Nelson, 1996], 349).

Question 5. In contrast to the rest Christ offers, the exorcised evil spirit (Luke 11:24) and the worshipers of the beast (Revelation 14:11) *cannot* find rest.

Question 6. IVP's *Dictionary of Biblical Imagery* includes this helpful information about the usage of "yoke" in the Bible:

> The yoke is an image of subjection, service or bondage (just as a yoked donkey or ox is in service to its owner) or an image of joining (just as two animals are joined together by means of a yoke)....As a symbol of legitimate discipline in a person's life, bearing the yoke in one's youth "is good," on a par with waiting quietly for the salvation of the Lord (Lam 3:26-27). The supreme example is Jesus' turning his paradoxical rhetoric to the yoke as a form of good subjection to him. ("Yoke," *Dictionary of Biblical Imagery*, 975)

Question 8. *Gentle* (or *meek*) is one of the qualities of the "blessed" in Matthew 5:5 and was predicted of the Messiah (Matthew 21:5). *Humble* carries the idea of "low-lying" but always in a positive sense in the New Testament.

STUDY 4. RENEWAL WITHIN DEFEAT. LUKE 24:13-35.

PURPOSE: To be reenergized by the reality of the risen and living Christ.

Question 2. Artistic depictions of the encounter on the Emmaus road usually portray these followers of Jesus as two men. Luke says only that one was a man named Cleopas (v. 18); the other is unidentified. Since they shared a home in Emmaus (v. 29), they could have been husband and wife or brother and sister.

Question 6. At this point we are not told how the two responded to the stranger's words, except that they invited him to stay with them. Perhaps they wanted to hear more, or perhaps they only extended customary hospitality as night was falling.

Question 7. Until now "they were kept from recognizing him" (v. 16), but now "their eyes were opened and they recognized him" (v. 31). There was divine timing in their recognition of who the stranger was. The fact that he immediately "disappeared from their sight" must have cinched the fact that their guest was no ordinary person.

STUDY 5. HELP WITHIN HOSTILITY. 2 CORINTHIANS 4:7-18.

PURPOSE: To take courage and comfort in Christ in the face of hostility from others.

Questions 2 and 3. John Wesley preached on the appropriateness of Paul's image of treasure in earthenware jars:

> The word is exquisitely proper, denoting both the brittleness of the vessels, and the meanness of the matter they are made of. It directly means, what we term earthenware; china, porcelain, and the like. How weak, how easily broken in pieces! Just such is the case with a holy Christian. We have the heavenly treasure in earthly, mortal, corruptible bodies.... God has done this, that "the excellency of the power might be of God, and not of us"; that it might be undeniably plain, to whom that excellent power belonged; that no flesh might glory in his sight." (John Wesley, *The Heavenly Treasure in Earthen Vessels* [Albany, OR: SAGE Software, 1996], 386-88)

Question 8. In verse 13 Paul quotes Psalm 116:10 from the Septuagint, the Greek translation of the Old Testament.

It is of great significance that Paul uses a quotation from the OT in order to emphasize his faith shared with the psalmist. His faith is in line with the faith of his ancestors; he stands in continuity with the faith of the OT writers. However, his faith is also faith in Jesus Christ. The early Christians are in continuity with the OT, but they believe in God who sent his Son, Jesus. The faith of the early Christians is bound to Jesus Christ; this is the new element in the faith that they share with, for example, the psalmist. (Peter Balla, "2 Corinthians," in *Commentary on the New Testament Use of the Old Testament*, ed. Greg K. Beale and D. A. Carson [Grand Rapids: Baker Academic, 2007], 765)

Note that Paul refers not only to hope of resurrected life someday, but to his current experience of preaching the gospel and caring for the church in Corinth.

STUDY 6. COURAGE WITHIN INJUSTICE. ACTS 16:16-40.

PURPOSE: To face injustice in a Christlike manner.

Question 3. N. T. Wright explains that the missionaries had entered the territory of

> strange spiritual forces, which seemed to be stirred up by a new gospel work, just as in [Acts] chapters 8 and 13. The ancient Greek world knew all about "divination," and people regularly went to places like Delphi to ask the priestess of Apollo for advice on everything from getting married to making war. Sometimes it seems that the system was merely a matter of cynical folk making a profit out of simple souls, both the ones asking the questions and the ones giving the "answer." But sometimes, as here, it seems to have been a case of someone, often a young woman, actually possessing some kind of prophetic spirit. And her "minders" were, of course, making a tidy profit out of her. . . .
>
> Which, of course, brought the second malevolent force into play. The profit motive. The girl's minders were suddenly as bereft of business as a fisherman whose boat has just sunk. Not for the last time, when the gospel suddenly impacts someone's trade, they turn nasty.
>
> And so they invoke the third force: religious and political prejudice. They dragged Paul and Silas before the magistrates. "These men are Jews," they shouted (which was of course true), "and they are advocating customs which *we Romans* ought not to adopt or observe" (which was of course half true). . . .
>
> The combination of religion, money and politics is asking for trouble, and Paul and Silas got it. Stripped, flogged and jailed, they discovered what happens to those who challenge the powers of the world with the power of the Name of Jesus. (N. T. Wright, *Acts for Everyone: Part Two*, 62-65)

Question 6. Keener says,

> Asking how to be saved is a motif in Luke-Acts (Lk 3:10; 10:25; 18:18; Acts 2:37); the jailer in this case may view Paul and Silas as representatives of the gods, who can "save/deliver/heal" (all

potentially implied in the same Greek word); more likely, he is familiar with their teaching of the one true God known in Judaism. (Keener, *IVP Bible Background Commentary: New Testament*, 370)

Question 8. Again Keener observes that

By waiting until after the beating (cf. 22:29) to inform the authorities that they were citizens, the missionaries had placed the magistrates themselves in an awkward legal position: now the magistrates, not the missionaries, are forced to negotiate. Reports of their deed could even disqualify them from office and (in theory, at least) deprive Philippi of its status as a Roman colony. This strategy would help secure the future safety of the fledgling Christian community. (Keener, *IVP Bible Background Commentary: New Testament*, 370-71)

STUDY 7. RESTORATION WITHIN RUIN. MARK 5:1-20.

PURPOSE: To grow in faith that Christ is strong enough to deal with the most negative and oppressive forces that threaten us.

Question 5. Professor Graham Twelftree says,

From Mark's perspective the importance of Jesus' dealing with the demons can be gauged by noting that one of Jesus' first public acts is an exorcism. And of his thirteen healing stories the largest single category is that of exorcism (1:21-28; 5:1-20; 7:24-30; 9:14-29). Then Mark heightens the importance of Jesus' exorcisms through the summaries of Jesus' ministry (1:32-34; 3:11-12). . . . In confronting the demons Jesus is empowered by the Spirit and is doing battle against Satan (3:22-30). Through the exorcisms (1:24, 27) and confrontations with the demons (1:34; 3:11-12, 23-27; 5:7) and the demonic (4:41), the Jesus of Mark is shown to be the Son of God (3:11; 5:7). (Graham H. Twelftree, "Demon, Devil, Satan," *Dictionary of Jesus and the Gospels* [Downers Grove, IL: IVP Academic, 1992], 169-70)

Question 6. Note the irony in the contrast between the disciples' confusion and the demons' certainty about who Jesus is. When Jesus calmed the storm the preceding night, the disciples asked each other in bewilderment, "Who is this?" (Mark 4:41). The demons immediately cried out, "Jesus, Son of the Most High God" (v. 7).

The best explanation of the phrase "son of God" here is that it refers to Jesus as Messiah. Those who believed in a coming Messiah regarded him as the one who would judge the world and put all wrongs to rights. That is why the demons instantly suspect they are in trouble. If the Messiah is here, the end of their time of freedom has come. They are, in a sense, quite right: Jesus has indeed come to put the forces of evil to flight, and what happens to these demons—entering pigs and driving them into the lake—is a sign of what Jesus will do, in his death and resurrection, with all evil of whatever sort. (N. T. Wright, *Matthew for Everyone, Part One: Chapters 1–15* [Louisville, KY: Westminster John Knox Press, 2004], 94-95)

The drowning of the pigs bothers some readers of this passage. In our society, where meat is neatly prepackaged and where animal sacrifice is unknown, it is easy to sentimentalize the fate of the pigs. Walter Kaiser writes,

We also see the economics of the story, while the Gospel writers were far more concerned with God's present provision (Mk 6:7-13) and future treasure in heaven than in preserving economic security now. Furthermore, we see the violence done to animals, while the Gospel writers were concerned with the violent destructive behavior of demons and their effects upon human beings. ... [From the perspective of the Gospel writers] the pigs are not the issue—they are unclean—and the townsfolk miss the point when they see only their loss of pigs and fail to see the delivered man. Indeed, the pigs plunging into the sea may suggest that the unclean land had been freed of the unclean spirits with the removal of the unclean animals; but the people do not want salvation, preferring pigs. (Kaiser et al., *Hard Sayings of the Bible*, 372-74)

Question 9. N. T. Wright explains,

Everywhere else Jesus went, people asked him to stay with them, and brought him more sick people to cure. Curiously, the people of Gadara regarded him with fear, and begged him to leave their district. Was it because they were Gentiles, and were anxious about the Jewish Messiah coming to them? Was it because they were frightened that if he started sending pigs into the lake he might cause other destruction of property and livestock? We don't know.

What we do know is that wherever Jesus went, people were in awe of him. There was no sense, as in much of the world today, that he was just one teacher among others, one religious leader to be coolly appraised. He was a force to be reckoned with. You might follow him, or you might be scared stiff of him, but you couldn't ignore him. That is the Jesus we must follow today, the Jesus we must make known in the world. (Wright, *Matthew*, 95)

STUDY 8. BELONGING WITHIN LONELINESS. 2 TIMOTHY 4:9-22.

PURPOSE: To realize more deeply that we belong to Christ.

Question 2. When Paul writes "Get Mark and bring him with you," this is apparently John Mark, who started traveling with Paul and Barnabas but abandoned them in midjourney (Acts 12:25–13:13). Paul and Barnabas parted company in a dispute over whether to trust him again (Acts 15:36-41). By this late time in his life, Paul has been reconciled with Mark and considers him a valuable partner in ministry.

Question 3. John Stott observes,

When our spirit is lonely, we need friends. When our body is cold, we need clothing. When our mind is bored, we need books. These are the natural needs of mortal men and women. . . . We must not, then, deny our humanity or frailty, or pretend that we are made of other stuff than dust. (John Stott, *The Message of 2 Timothy*, Bible Speaks Today [Downers Grove, IL: InterVarsity Press, 1973], 119-21)

Question 7. While Paul wants Alexander to be repaid for the harm he did, Paul leaves it up to the Lord to execute judgment. He expresses hope that the Lord will not judge those who deserted him at his first defense.

STUDY 9. EMPATHY WITHIN FALTERING. HEBREWS 4:14-5:10.

PURPOSE: To grow in trust that Jesus our high priest knows and understands our weaknesses, even as he powerfully represents us to God.

Question 1. Professor Rodney Duke says,

> Through their instructions and rituals, the priests warned Israel how its waywardness, intentional and unintentional, polluted God's dwelling and hindered God's presence in their covenant relationship. Individuals and community alike were called to be "clean" and pure before God. Moreover, through the priestly role, Israel saw that Yahweh's graciousness was not limited to mighty historical acts and the anointed leadership of key individuals. God had provided the means of removing the pollution, of purifying the unclean person and of restoring the divinely intended order. It was through the priesthood that this message of grace was mediated. (Rodney K. Duke, "Priests, Priesthood," *Dictionary of the Old Testament: Pentateuch*, ed. T. Desmond Alexander and David W. Baker [Downers Grove, IL: InterVarsity Press, 2003], 654)

Question 3. *The Hard Sayings of the Bible* points out that we human beings face the same kinds of tests Jesus faced: whether or not to trust God and refuse to compromise with evil. Because Jesus has successfully met these tests, he can help us in our times of temptation.

> A person who failed a test is hardly the one to coach another on how to prepare for the test. Jesus took the very same test as we do, indeed, a more intense form of the very same test. But he passed. He "was without sin." He did not fail in any way. As a result he can in fact respond with true sympathy to human beings now suffering under testing, for he truly "feels with," having himself felt the same pain and impulses. He can also show by example the successful way through the test. (Kaiser et al., *Hard Sayings*, 680)

Question 4. According to the *Dictionary of Biblical Imagery*,

> Perfection of the priesthood awaited Jesus. He is the perfect high priest, being the divine Son of God (Heb 7:16) who alone possesses

sinless perfection, but yet being a brother to humanity through his incarnation (Heb 2:11-18). In contrast to the law-ordained, sin-tainted, perpetual and numerous sacrifices of the OT priests, Jesus was the sinless offerer of his sinless self once and for all on behalf of his people (Heb 7–10, esp., e.g., Heb 7:27; 9:12, 28; 10:10, 14). He is the high priest par excellence because he made himself the sacrifice par excellence. Not only in his offering but also in his place of service, he perfected the priesthood, for he entered into the most holy place in heaven to make atonement (Heb 9:23-24). ("Priest," *Dictionary of Biblical Imagery*, 663)

Question 5. J. A. Motyer says,

When Hebrews (6:20–7:28) uses Melchizedek in order to show that the Lord Jesus is a true priest though without Aaronic ancestry, it is the fulfillment of a line of truth reaching back through David to Abraham. Jesus is indeed the true Melchizedek of whom Abram met the prototype, David was the foreshadowing and of whom Zechariah spoke. (J. A. Motyer, "Psalm 110," *New Bible Commentary, 21st Century Edition*, ed. D. A. Carson et al. [Downers Grove, IL: InterVarsity Press, 1994], 562)

Question 7. According to the *Hard Sayings of the Bible,*

It is one thing to obey when there is no resistance; it is another thing to obey when that very obedience will bring you pain. Before the Incarnation, who resisted the Son? Only in his life on earth did he suffer for his obedience. In other words, there are some things that even God can experience only by becoming a human being with all of our human limitations. Obedience in the face of suffering is one of them. This in turn brought Jesus to perfection, which has the sense of "maturity" or "fulfillment." That is, through obedience in the face of intense suffering, Jesus was able to complete or fulfill his mission, namely to become the source or basis of eternal salvation (versus a temporal deliverance) to those who in turn obey him. This completed mission is the basis for his present high priesthood. (Kaiser et al., *Hard Sayings*, 680-81)

STUDY 10. MERCY WITHIN FAILURE. JOHN 18:15-18, 25-27; 21:15-19.

PURPOSE: To find hope that Christ is merciful to us in our failures.

Question 6. The "relative of the man whose ear Peter had cut off" (v. 26) refers to John 18:10-11. When Jesus was arrested in Gethsemane, Peter, who apparently came to the garden armed with a sword, struck at the high priest's servant Malchus and severed his ear. Jesus sharply reprimanded Peter for his action. Luke reports that Jesus touched the ear and healed it (Luke 22:50-51).

Question 9. The Greek word for "love" in Jesus' first two questions is the word for divine love; in the third question it is the word for affectionate friendship. Keener explains:

> The two Greek words for "love" here are used interchangeably elsewhere in John and generally in the literature of this period; the point is not (against some interpreters) in the different terms, but that love for Jesus must be demonstrated by obedience to his call and service to his people. (Keener, *IVP Bible Background Commentary: New Testament*, 319)

Questions 11 and 12. Donald Guthrie observes,

> The fact that Peter was clearly forgiven by Jesus and given new responsibilities, amounting to apostleship, despite his total denial of his Lord, can give genuine hope to Christians today who feel that they have denied Jesus and that this is unforgiveable. He calls only for our repentance and our love. (Donald Guthrie, "John," in D. A. Carson et al., *New Bible Commentary*, 1065)

Dale and Sandy Larsen are freelance writers living in Rochester, Minnesota. They have written more than forty books and Bible study guides, including the LifeBuilder Bible Studies Hosea: God's Persistent Love, Faith: Depending on God, Questions God Asks *and* Couples of the Old Testament.

Printed and bound by CPI Group (UK) Ltd, Croydon, CR0 4YY

27/03/2025

14649113-0001